Contact the author:
www.joshuabestcreative.com | twitter: @joshuabest
joshuabestcreative@gmail.com | instagram: joshuadavidbest

Contact the publisher:
Unprecedented Press LLC - 495 Sleepy Hollow Ln, Holland, MI 49423
www.unprecedentedpress.com | info@unprecedentedpress.com
twitter: @UnprecdntdPress | instagram: unprecedentedpress

ISBN-10:0-9861931-9-4
ISBN-13:978-0-9861931-9-4

Printed in the United States of America
Ingram Printing & Distribution, 2017
Edited by Rose White

First Edition

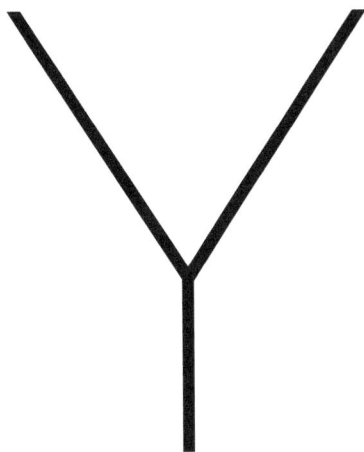

Y

THE WORKBOOK

Companion to
Y - CHRISTIAN
MILLENNIAL
MANIFESTO

Joshua Best

Un
Pd

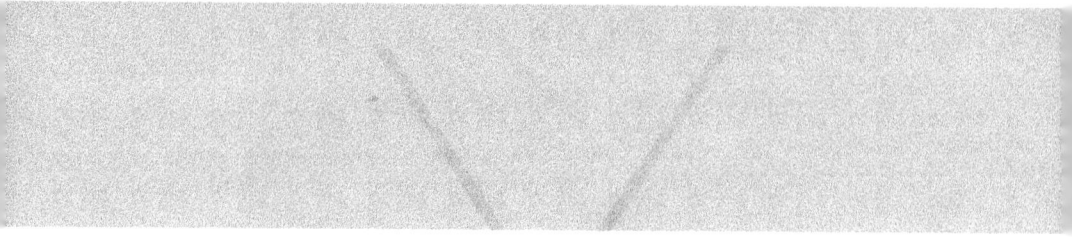

TABLE OF CONTENTS

PREFACE

When writing *Y - Christian Millennial Manifesto*, I found myself outlining some of my concerns about the Millennial generation. I highlighted some weaknesses we need to overcome, in addition to the strengths we need to amplify. As I was going through the material, I found it impossible to present the problems without providing some suggestions for how to solve them. I wrote all of my suggestions into the first draft of the book, but they were so practical that they seemed out of place in the manifesto. When I took them all out, I realized there were enough for a companion workbook, which you're now reading.

If you haven't read the main book yet, I suggest doing that before going through the workbook because some of my practical applications won't make sense without first understanding the context. This workbook is divided into three sections, and they correspond with three chapters from the manifesto:

Turn On Silent, Sticking To It, and Holy Devotion. If you want to cherry pick, you don't have to read the whole book. Just read those three chapters, and this workbook will make sense for the most part.

My wife is very smart. She reads roughly 100 books a year, and she has a Masters degree in English. She also has a lot of other stellar traits. She's organized, loyal, and very determined, but she would never claim to be entreprenuerial. If my marriage has taught me anything, it's that people are different. As a creative person, I only need to read a couple sentences and my mind starts wandering with possible applications, but not everyone is like me. That's the main reason I've put together this workbook. I want to provide you with some tools. Heaven forbid, you read my book and realize you need to change but don't know how. That's why it's my distinct privilege to provide you with some ideas and suggestions for how to overcome in the areas that are toughest for Christian Millennials.

This workbook contains questions with space provided for your answers, and actionable steps for you to take right away. I will ask you to seek God, hear his voice, and make real changes. If you're ready for that, you're ready for this workbook. Dig in!

"It's easy to become so busy doing great things in life, that we run out of time and forget to ask God."

– Cindy Best
Church leader & my amazing mother

GET OFF THE GRID

When was the last time you went for a walk to simply admire God's creation? When was the last time you went somewhere without your phone? A week? A month? A year? We often remark about the challenge of hearing God's voice, but we continue to allow distraction to get in our way. God gave us eyes to see his beauty, ears to hear his voice, a nose to smell his presence, and a mind to meditate on his Word. God is able to speak to us through creation in a powerful way, and if we don't give him that permission, then we have nothing to complain about. Do yourself a favor: stop reading now and go for a walk. Find a forest, a beach, or a local trail. Go, and leave your phone, your iPad, or your laptop at home. It can be a walk or a hike. You could even lay down in a field. I recently took an hour to lay down at a riverbank. I looked up at the sky, and I talked to God. More importantly, I let him talk to me. He spoke to me about my character, my relationships, and his own nature. Go. Do what you have to do to be with God. I guarantee that when you slow down and listen, he will speak.

ACTION STEP:

Go for a walk in nature to hear God's voice. Leave your devices in your car, and don't Instagram your experience.

FOLLOW-UP QUESTIONS:

1) Where did you go?

_____

_____

2) Were you successful in leaving your devices behind? How difficult was it?

_____

_____

_____

3) Did Gid speak to you? If so, what did he say?

_____

_____

_____

_____

_____

_____

"Start with the mustard seed.
It will grow big, but be willing
to start at seed level."

– Jeff Johnson
   Leader, missionary & father of 4 Millennials

TURN ON SILENT

CAPTURE WISDOM

Paul writes in Romans 12:3 (NIV), "Do not think of yourself more highly than you ought, but rather think of yourself with sober judgment." In other words, stop being so proud. One of the problems with pride is it prevents you from recognizing you're proud. The characteristics of this shortcoming disguise the shortcoming from you. It means that you might not think I'm talking to you, but I probably am.

Confidence in your identity is important, but not to the degree that you think you have it all figured out. There's always someone who knows more than you. Even the smartest people in the world could stand to learn a thing or two from someone. As Christians in God's family, we're never above input from our fellow believers – that's the way the body of Christ works. We need to start intentionally learning from people who have more experience than we do. If you can think of the elderly people in your life as a gift or a resource, you'll grow much faster into a mature Christian.

Take a moment to think about your grandparents. If you don't have any, think about the older friends in your life. If you don't have any of those, you might need to read the chapter in the main book called *Be Church*. These people carry tremendous value for young adults. Not only have they experienced the same things on a human level, but they have the benefit of hindsight. They've observed their parents' generation, their own generation, our parents' generation, and our generation. They've watched how we respond differently to world events and social development. That means they can easily spot unhealthy behaviors, and they know where certain decisions will lead.

These elderly people won't be here forever. I'm not trying to be morbid or foreboding, but I want you to understand the urgency. The limited time we have with these individuals makes it that much more important for us to intentionally ask them the tough questions.

ACTION STEP:

Think of a person over 60. Send them a message right now, and see if they can meet you for lunch or coffee this week. Tell them you'll pay.

When you meet with them, ask them questions about things they see in you and things they think you need to change. Then, listen carefully to their answers. Capture the responses by recording them with your phone, taking notes, and reciting their feedback to your friends and family. Really listen. This will ensure the input into your life and the life of your children is not lost, but is put into practice. I guarantee they won't be embarrassed, and they will be honored to impart their wisdom to you. I have made this my habit for the past ten years, and many of my encounters are published in this book. I can tell you from experience that not only are they willing to share with inquisitive young people, but most elderly people are, in fact, honored by the opportunity to affect the future. It will encourage them to know that our generation has individuals who have not succumbed to thinking they have it all figured out.

FOLLOW-UP QUESTIONS:

1) Name two things you admire about their perspective on life:

_____

_____

2) How can you apply these to your life this week?

_____

_____

"I want Millennials to find a genuine love for God and his people because agape love translates into true righteousness, peace, and joy."

– Stephen Best
Pastor of River Run Fellowship & my loving dad

GAMIFY LIFE

f you struggle with keeping your attention on something you've committed to, here are some millennial-friendly suggestions for how you can stick to it:

Try taking a step back from your commitment in question and see the big picture. Now, try to verbalize why you first agreed to be involved. Narrow it right down the purpose or reason behind your investment in this area of your life. Write it down in a concise sentence or two below:

_____

_____

_____

Next, think of this committment as a mission and give it a name. My background is in branding, and I find that naming or branding a personal initiative makes it feel more exciting and more like something I would want to do. For example, my wife and I call our budget meetings "Hour of Order," and I once made a health goal which I called "25 in 50," which referred to losing 25 pounds in 50 days. Your name might be "Operation: Open Doors" or "The Amazing Debt Free Endeavor." Whatever name you come up with, write it here:

_____

_____

Now that you've given your mission a flashy title, break it down into large chunks. These are like the levels in a video game or chapters in a book. If your commitment is college, then maybe these chunks are semesters. If it's a job you don't like, perhaps these are seasons of the year. Next, write two or three bullet points for each chunk that describes what you want to accomplish during the timeframe. These details are like describing the challenges you face in a video game. For instance, level four is the dungeon level. It includes picking a lock, getting past the guards, and beating the boss.

1	_____
	_____
	_____
	_____

2

_____
_____
_____
_____

3

_____
_____
_____
_____

4

_____
_____
_____
_____

ACTION STEP:

Make a poster and put it up in your house to remind you of your mission and why you're doing it. Cross off each section as you complete it. You'll feel encouraged as you make progress.

"I want to see courage
and determination,
which I think has been
lacking in Millennials."

– Dave Roberts
Pastor from Wales, father in the faith

STICKING TO IT
ROMANTICIZE MINUTIA

As Millennials, we're not accustomed to applying ourselves the way other generations have been. Repetitive or boring tasks aren't quite our cup of tea. We've been raised to pursue our dreams, we've been told not to do anything unless it makes us happy, and we've gotten used to getting what we want. As you may have noticed by now, life is not about you or me. That's why we Millennials need to embrace monotony. We can't despise difficulty. Imagine where you'd be without overcoming challenges. We're better people for going through difficult circumstances in our lives. James tells us to think of our trials as pure joy (James 1:2). That scripture continues saying, "the testing of your faith produces perseverance." It says this perseverence is needed to make us fully mature.

Write down three monotonous tasks you are required to do at work, school, or around the home?

1
_____

2
_____

3
_____

One way to curb your distaste for mindless detail is to glorify God on the journey. Next time you find yourself at work or at school or doing a chore that you hate (but you're committed to), try imagining yourself in a dramatic movie scene. It could be a sports movie like *Remember The Titans* or a biopic like *Erin Brockovich*. Those types of movies highlight individuals who persevered through difficult situations and succeeded against all odds. If your life was an inspirational biopic or sports movie, what would you call it?

_____

_____

The only difference between your story and the stories on the screen is that yours doesn't have a soundtrack. So here's an opportunity to use your great Millennial imagination. Try adding a soundtrack to your chores or picturing yourself in slow motion. It sounds silly, but it works. Just ask a runner. Any runner who tells you they don't pretend to be in *Chariots Of Fire* on that last stretch is lying to you. Why else do runners listen to music? It's a way to romanticize the minutia of each and every step. It's a way to elevate difficulty, remember its importance, and make sure it gets done.

What song would be your slow motion song?

_____

What song would be your preparation montage song?

_____

What song would be your victory song that leads into the movie credits?

_____

ACTION STEP:

Once you decide, see if you can actually build a playlist with songs that you can listen to while doing your difficult task. If you can't, just imagine it, and listen to them when you get home.

"[Millennials] are more open than we were. When I was twenty, there was a lot we didn't talk about. But every area in life is open to them."

– Diane Soper
Respected mother & grandmother in faith

SHARE THE BURDEN

Believers aren't designed to endure difficulty alone. God's plan for the church is to have a functioning community that supports each other and bears each other's burdens. As brothers and sisters in Christ, our job is to be here for one another in difficult times. A 60-year old may not struggle with commitment, but Millennials do. And that's nothing to be embarrassed about.

If you know you're prone to flaking out or giving up too soon, I encourage you to reach out to someone in your church. If you ask them, they'll keep you accountable. Don't forget – there's power in numbers. The Bible says that one can put 1000 to flight but two can put 10,000 to flight (Deuteronomy 32:30). That's kingdom math. It may not make sense to your mind, but something happens in the spiritual world when believers agree together. "Again, truly I tell you that if two of you on earth agree about anything they ask for, it will be done for them by my Father in heaven" (Matthew 18:19, NIV).

List two close friends to be accountable to for this challenge:

1

_____

2

_____

ACTION STEP:

Text your two close friends now and ask them to meet up. Share your struggle to persevere so they can encourage and challenge you.

In addition to personal accountability, another way to share the burden of commitment is to share with your social network. This is one way that Millennials can take advantage of their natural inclinations. We are avid sharers in the social space. Take advantage of the platform to announce changes in your life or share successes. This is one of the purest uses of the space – to lean on your friends for encouragement when you need it.

ACTION STEP:

When you reach one of your goals or you succeed at an endeavor, share the good news with your social media network so your friends can celebrate with you.

"Jesus was radical, and all the disciples followed him. They didn't have a guide, except for Jesus himself. And that's what we're supposed to have – Jesus himself."

– Diane Soper
   Respected mother & grandmother in faith

BE AN ALIEN

Once you've turned away from what you were doing and changed direction, you can focus on building better habits into your life. Traditionally, separation from the world meant joining a monastary. Truly, those devout individuals live a life that is devoted to God and void of distraction – or at least that's the goal. But instead of suggesting you become a monk or a nun (we can't all do that), I suggest becoming an alien.

In fact, the Bible uses the analogy of extraterrestrial life in 1 Peter 2:11, NASB, saying we are aliens and strangers on earth. Obviously, it doesn't mean that we're Klingons, Wookies, or something from science fiction. It means we're citizens of heaven, and our true home is with Jesus. I think we should embrace that. As we consider how we ought to live – holy and devoted to God – remembering our true nationality can really help.

Superman is a noble hero who uses his powers to help the human race, but if you think about it, Superman doesn't fully embrace his identity as an alien. He was born on the planet Krypton, but he hides his identity from the people around him. We often do the same thing. We want the benefit of power that comes with a faith-filled life, but when we go back to work, we just want to fit in. Like Superman, we want to be just like everyone else. And that's the problem – we're not like everyone else.

I think we need to be more like X-Men than Superman. The X-Men stopped hiding their identities, and they came out of the shadows. They announced to the world that mutants exist and they let their presence be known. We should do the same with the light inside us. We should be proud to be different. We should vocalize our godly choices and decisions instead of hiding them. If you start embracing your true identity, it will give you permission to be different. Fear of how we look to our peers can often dictate how we live. If your relationship with God is negatively affected by your relationship with people, then you've put those people above God. Decide today to own your identity. You'll find the oppressive shackles of conformity will simply fall away.

When we were saved, we were literally reborn from above. In the book *Realities Of The New Creation*, author E.W. Kenyon explains that salvation is the greatest miracle ever performed because the spirit within each of us was completely reborn in the likeness of God. Our nature was totally changed. Instead of having a sinful nature and origin, we now have a pure nature, and we have originated from Christ instead of Adam. Let's embrace what God's done for us by embracing our unique nature.

Name an activity, habit or friend that you know isn't good for you:

_____

What's the one thing you need to do to separate yourself?

_____

_____

Putting ourselves in the right situations helps us make good decisions, but the real test is in what we say. Jesus asked Peter, "Who do you say I am?" There comes a time when every believer must speak his or her beliefs out loud. Ask yourself if there is someone you need to make a bold statement to. It could be a friend who has a negative influence on you, or a boss who insists you work when you should be at church. What is it you need to tell them? Write it here:

_____

_____

_____

_____

"Be careful to keep worship authentic. Trends can come and go, but we must keep lifting up Christ and magnifying His name."

– Cindy Best
Church leader & my amazing mother

HOLY DEVOTION
LISTEN TO HYMNS

To move away from a "me" mentality, we have to find ways to focus on Christ. We also need to find ways to get a better picture of who he is. My most practical suggestion for quickly addressing your thought life is to find some old hymns and listen to them in your devotional time with God. Unlike some worship songs written today, old hymns don't usually shy away from the deep things of God. They were written during an era when people really understood the fear of the Lord. Believers in past centuries had a reverence and a respect for God that was second to none. Often, their fear led to guilt, and most times it wasn't paired with an understanding of God's grace. But that doesn't mean we can't learn from their strengths.

ACTION STEP:

Stop what you're doing and pull out your phone. Go to YouTube and search for one of the following songs. As it plays, let God speak to you about his power, his righteousness, and his jealousy. Let him show you that side of himself. Not just the loving dad, but Almighty God.

How Great Thou Art
What a Friend We Have in Jesus
There is Power in the Blood
Holy, Holy, Holy
Create in Me a Clean Heart

My grandfather Frederick's favorite hymn was "What A Friend We Have In Jesus." He even asked that we we sing it at his funeral. I heard it for the first time that day, and it brought me to tears. Not only did it remind me of his faith in the person of Jesus Christ, it grounded me in the practice of habitual prayer. Do me a favor – don't neglect these old songs. There's a reason they've been around for hundreds of years. Not all of them are perfectly in line with my exact doctrine. But if you listen to them with a humble ear, I have no doubt that you will find a new level of reverence for the Lord that will help you live a devoted life.

When you were listening to hymns, what did God say to you about himself? Write below what he revealed to you:

ABOUT THE AUTHOR

A Canadian living in Michigan, Joshua Best is a church pastor at The Point Church, a freelance art director in the advertising industry, and the founder of Unprecedented Press. He's a catalyst for change in church, family, and business.

Josh and his wife, April, have been leaders of the The Point Exchange, a young adult ministry in Grand Rapids, for over seven years. They are both passionate about seeing their generation pursue God with gusto. They currently serve God in Holland, Michigan and have two young children. Josh has written one other book in two volumes called *40 Shocking Facts for 40 Weeks of Pregnancy.*

E V E R Y O N E

global giving initiative

As we pursue our mission to help people get their voices and ideas out into the world, we realize that others are concerned with more pressing needs. Finding creativity in every person is important work, but getting food, shelter, and dignity to individuals must come first. That's why Unprecedented Press donates a portion of all book revenue to the Everyone Gobal Giving Initative whose goal is to meet the practical needs of individuals around the world and to share the love of Jesus. To learn more, visit *everyoneglobal.com*

Other titles from

Unprecedented Press

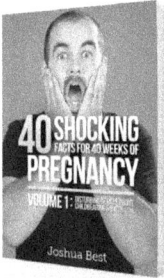

40 Shocking Facts for 40 Weeks
of Pregnancy - Volume 1:
*Disturbing Details about
Childbearing & Birth*

By Joshua Best

40 Shocking Facts for 40 Weeks
of Pregnancy - Volume 2:
*Terrifying Truths about Babies
& Breastfeeding*

By Joshua Best

She Can Laugh
*A Guide to Living Spiritually,
Emotionally & Physically Healthy*

By Melissa Lea Hughes

Once Upon A Year
*Experience a year in
the life of Finn*

By Joanna Lenau

www.ingramcontent.com/pod-product-compliance
Lightning Source LLC
Chambersburg PA
CBHW062153020426
42334CB00020B/2593